The Lifta Hamideh Ismail Legacy

By

Sue Hamideh

Progressive
RISING PHOENIX PRESS ®

Text Copyright © 2023 Sue Hamideh

Published 2023 by
Progressive Rising Phoenix Press, LLC,
www.progressiverisingphoenix.com

ISBN: 978-1-958640-38-8

Printed in the U.S.A.
1st Printing

Cover and Interior Photos provided by Sue Hamideh

Cover design by Amanda Thrasher

Book design by William Speir
Visit: http://www.williamspeir.com

Acknowledgements

I am forever grateful for the following persons for guidance, information, and translation during the preparation of this book.

The first is my beloved husband, Naji Othman Ali Hamideh, who preserved and shared written, pictorial, and verbal information during his lifetime and after he passed away.

The second person was one of my doctors for many years, Dr. Marianne Zinnate, as she encouraged me for several years to write my husband's family story down for future generations.

I would also like to thank Kamal Ismail and Sawsan Abusaad for sharing their families' information and history. I am forever grateful to each and every one of them and pray that I have done my best to preserve in some small way the amazing legacy that they have!

I'd also like to thank my nephew, Suleiman Hamideh, who resides in San Antonio. Suleiman spent many evenings after work translating writings on backs of photographs and letters, for which I am extremely grateful!

I dedicate this writing to:
Othman Ali Hamideh, son of Ali and Hafeetha
Hamideh,
Habiba Hamideh, daughter of Mohammed and
Ezyah Hamideh,
and their progeny, hoping they will carry the mantle
of character, faith, stamina, and resilience that they
displayed in the harshest of circumstances!

Chapter 1
The Hamideh Family Genealogy

A long time ago, in the late 19th century, Ali Hamideh from Lifta village in Palestine married Hafeetha Hamideh from Betine village. Their marriage produced six children: Sulieman, Othman, Othmana, Younis, Alia, and Yosef.

They lived in an area (Lifta) that was a beautiful hillside village with very fertile land. So, they grew and harvested crops and prospered there.

* * *

In 1913, when Othman was a young man, he boarded a ship from Palestine to travel to the United States. That trip took nearly three weeks. After arriving in New York, he eventually made his way to Butte, Montana. While there, he opened a dry goods store with a partner. From what we know, that partner was a Jewish man.

Othman Ali Hamideh and his Jewish business partner

After living in America for thirteen years, his family missed him and wanted him to come home—and that, he did. Once he was back home in Lifta, Palestine, his parents encouraged him to find a wife to marry. The daughter of Mohammed Hamideh and Ezyah Hamideh was to become his bride. Her name was Habiba Hamideh, and they became husband and wife. They then started their own family, and Othman began working in farming and other areas to provide for their family.

Their marriage produced six children. Their names, in birth order, were Aisha, Mohammed, Havtha, Omar, Naji, and Ahmed. Aisha was the first of the siblings to marry. Later her son, Mohammed, married Omar Hamideh's daughter, Sufa.

From what I have researched, Othman was a man before his time, and he was creative in trying various avenues to provide for his family's future. Not only were day-to-day essentials part of that goal, but education was very important to him. His desire to be able to provide opportunity and education for their children was foremost a priority.

He prospered not only with farming, but other areas as well—a coffee shop and other opportunities.

* * *

Then in 1947–1948, what was called "The Palestinian Exodus" began. It was actually the Jewish army and some illegal Jewish groups using fear, as well as other tactics, to force Palestinians to flee for the safety of their families. Therefore, in 1948, Othman and his wife Habiba, along with their children, fled to Bethlehem for safety.

Their living conditions were terrible and unclean. One of their young sons, Naji, contracted malaria while there and was critically ill for a few weeks. Thankfully, he survived. Then their dear

3

mother, Habiba, became seriously ill and passed away while they were homeless in Bethlehem.

In 1950, the family migrated to Jordan, as the grandparents had some property there. Once again, Othman began with one truck hauling gravel to provide for his family. The maternal grandmother and the older sister, Havtha, helped care for the younger boys.

Othman Hamideh shown in a newspaper clipping from Amman, Jordan, in 1952. He was recycling glass.

Othman worked hard and was innovative enough to try various ways to earn money to care for his family. At one point in the 1950s, he was recycling glass to make bottles for a grape juice

4

factory in Amman. How innovative and what faith he showed.

Othman and his brother, Younis, built a house together for their families in Amman, Jordan. At the same time, he was hauling gravel and rocks for excavation purposes.

He began with one truck that eventually grew to a fleet of trucks and dozens of employees. His innovative ideas and his continued faith brought successes. The name of his company was Othman Hamideh and Sons.

He also believed in education and wanted to be able to afford a quality education for his children, especially for his two youngest sons, as the others were already grown. His middle son, Omar, worked alongside his father in the family business. Eventually, Othman was able to provide a quality education for his two youngest sons at a private school in Amman, Jordan.

While attending this prestigious school, on March 1,1956, Naji Hamideh and his entire senior class attended a demonstration celebrating King Hussein pushing Glubb Pasha and his troops out of Jordan.

All the while, Othman was working and raising his children; he spoke some English and told them stories of America. From what his son Naji said, their father loved pancakes and cold showers while living in America.

Mohammed, the oldest son of Othman, came to America in 1952. Sometime in the 1950s he, his Uncle Yusef, and his cousin Issa Ismail opened a cafe/coffee shop in Fort Worth, Texas, called "The Grand Café."

It was during this time that Naji Hamideh graduated from the private school in Amman. His desire was to come to the United States to pursue a college education. His brother, Mohammed, sent him an application for Texas Christian University in Fort Worth, Texas.

Within three weeks, Naji received his acceptance and was on his way a few weeks later to Fort Worth, Texas. It was in 1958 when he arrived. He began his collegiate career at Texas Christian University (TCU) in 1959 (see essay at end).

TCU was a very progressive school in working with their international students and introducing them to the university and to the Fort Worth community. Each international student had a sponsor family or couple from Fort Worth to aid them in getting to know the people and the city. A doctor and his wife were Naji's sponsors.

Naji also was elected president of the International Friendship Club at TCU and served in that office for a few years. In 1963, Naji graduated with his bachelor's degree in economics with a minor in sociology. He decided to continue on at TCU to pursue a master's degree in economics.

His brother Mohammed, by that time, had returned home to Amman, Jordan, and was getting married and starting a family there.

Naji still had an uncle and cousins in the area. He spent the next couple years working on his master's thesis, "The Functional Analysis of the Economic Development of Kuwait." It was quite interesting and informational.

This was also a most difficult time for Naji. While completing his master's thesis, he received word that his father, Othman, had passed away. Naji was unable to attend the funeral, as he was in the United States.

* * *

Upon achieving this educational goal in 1965, he decided that he needed to gain some work experience. During his search, he came across a management training opportunity in a family-owned department store in downtown Fort Worth. The company was named Leonard's Department Store. Naji completed the training program and was offered a management position, which he accepted.

One day, after he had been working there for some time, in walks an energetic, loquacious young lady. She was a new employee but at that moment was a customer shopping. Thus began the fairy tale.

The young lady noticed an accent and asked Naji where he was from and about his family. Sue Nodler was a management trainee in the store. Therefore, they became acquainted as coworkers and friends. The rest, as they say, was history.

They had a beautiful relationship and were married not too long after, maybe a year and a half. When they knew they were going to marry, Naji wanted to go back to Jordan to tell his family personally what his intentions were. Most all of his family had married distant relatives or persons from the same village where they lived. Sue totally understood and respected the fact that it was important for him to do that. And he did. He was gone for several weeks. She actually thought it was a beautiful thing that he had so much love and respect for his family.

His family loved and respected him also and wished him the best happiness. When he came back, they began making plans for their wedding. And he began a new career working in the insurance business. They were married in Fort Worth in the Egyptian Room at the Worth Hotel. Many friends and family members were with them to celebrate. Naji's sponsor couple from his time at TCU were in attendance as well.

It was a wonderful thing that they both had such strong support from their friends and families.

* * *

Naji with his wife Sue, son Farris, daughter Carima, and two grandsons, Jaxson and Jace, receiving the Human Relations Award from the city of Fort Worth, Texas

They became close and well loved by her family and his.

In 1975, they made their first family trip to the

Middle East to visit family. While there, they traveled to Jerusalem to visit extended family, and the village, Lifta, where Naji was born, and visited the cemetery where his parents, Othman and Habiba, were buried.

It was the first time that Naji had visited since his father passed away in 1965. He was studying at TCU and finishing his master's thesis at the time. Naji was also very active in interfaith groups and various volunteer agencies in the Fort Worth community.

Following a tornado in Fort Worth, he volunteered with the Red Cross, going door-to-door to make certain citizens were safe and had water. In 2005, Naji was awarded the Human Relations Award by the city council of Fort Worth.

* * *

He and Sue have three children: Farris, Carima, and Deanna. They also have five grandchildren: Ansley, Ashlyn, Jaxson, Jace, and Farris.

Several of Naji's relatives moved to the Dallas area for economic opportunities. But Naji loved Fort Worth and remained on the west side of the Dallas-Fort Worth area.

His Uncle Yousef was in the area for some time; he was married, working, and his oldest children were born there. He then lived in Jordan for some years, but he came back some time later and remained here.

His cousins Issa, Hassan, and Kamal Ismail all were in the area at that time and remained there, living and working as entrepreneurs in their respective vocations. Kamal Ismail started in Fort Worth as a tailor for a very nice men's clothing store. He married and moved to Dallas and has been quite a successful entrepreneur in the clothing retail and tailoring business. His brothers came to the area and have also been successful entrepreneurs. And all have been active in their communities. They all had learned tailoring skills from their father and or older brothers.

Furthermore, their uncle and some older brothers became entrepreneurs in grocery or related business ventures. Each of the family members valued education and continued the tradition of making that a priority for their children and future generations.

Chapter 2
Lifta

Lifta is a beautiful hillside village on the outskirts of Jerusalem. It has been called "The Palestinian Pompeii." Othman Ali Hamideh and all of his children were born in Lifta.

The ruins of the Village of Lifta

Lifta is on the northwest side of Jerusalem and has been an active village for centuries. It was naturally a fertile land and, as a result, was inhabited and the land was rich for agricultural purposes. It is located on a scenic hillside and blessed with a stream of water supply. Therefore, it was ideal for growing and harvesting crops and growing trees.

The village was rich with olive, fig, apricot, plum, almond, and pomegranate trees, plus fields of peas, spinach, peas, and beans. Over a door in one of the rock (stone) houses was a sign saying, "The people of the village cut the stones and built the houses themselves."

The village culture was very much like a family. The mosque was a major center in the village. And there was a school for children in the mosque. It is believed to be one of the first in Jerusalem area.

Lifta, due to its perfect authenticity and state of preservation as a village, provided a unique example of the traditional village life that existed there.

Lifta has been named as one of twenty-five endangered sites on the 2018 World Monuments Watch List. Lifta is a unique site for historical as well as archeological significance. In 1959, Lifta was also classified as a nature reserve. It's very important that Lifta is preserved for historical, cultural, and archeological significance. Also, the natural beauty of that hillside area is unique.

There actually is a Lifta Society in the Dallas

area with a nice center, located in Garland, Texas. Lifta women were also well known for their beautiful garments with dazzling embroidery detail. The Hamideh, Ismail, and Abusaad families all have their roots in the Lifta village in Jerusalem in Palestine.

* * *

It was absolutely necessary when compiling the legacy of the Hamideh family from Lifta to include the legacy of the Ismail family. Likewise, the Abusaad family is so very closely connected to the Hamideh and Ismail families as well. All of the families were from Lifta.

The first marriage union of the Hamideh and Ismail families from Lifta was the daughter of Ali Hamideh and Hafeetha Abdul Hafeez from Betine (another village). Her name was Othmana. She became the wife of Abrihim Ismail and that was the beginning of a generational familial connection between these two Palestinian families.

The marriage of Abrihim Ismail and Othmana Hamideh produced two sons and one daughter. The sons were named Issa Ismail and Hassan Ismail and the daughter was named Jamila Ismail, which means beautiful.

Othmana contracted a long-term illness and was

in a care facility for some time. Therefore, Abrihim Ismail married again, and his second wife was named Latifa Ameen Khalaf. They started a family and eventually had to leave Lifta, as they were forced out.

Their children were Lutfi, Ahmed, Iasha, Kamal, Nahada, Mohammed, and Awni. These children lost their mother at young ages due to health issues. Their father was a tailor and trained his sons in that skillset. They each worked hard and became successful.

In those times, it was customary for men to marry cousins or other distant family members. For example, Ahmed married Iasha Hamideh's daughter, Samira. Likewise, Omar Hamideh married Iasha, the Daughter of Ibrahim Ismail. Kamal Ismail married Fatima Hamideh, the daughter of Yousef Hamideh, the youngest son of Othman Ali Hamideh. And there were many more marital connections of the families.

Likewise, the Abusaad family were cousins as well and had marriages with members of the Ismail and Hamideh families. Issa Ismail was the first member of their family to come to the United States. Then his brother Hassan followed him. Issa was already married to Seham Hamideh, and they were residing in Fort Worth. His brother Hassan then came to reside with his brother and his brother's family. The following year their brother Kamal came to Fort Worth. Kamal Ismail, Hassan Ismail, and Naji Hamideh then found an apartment and resided together in Fort Worth. Naji Hamideh was working at Leonard's Department Store in downtown Fort Worth following the completion of his master's degree at TCU. Kamal Ismail began working as a tailor in an upscale men's clothing store in Fort Worth named Clyde Campbell. Hassan also worked in his own sales business.

It was not too long after that when Naji met the young lady who was to become his wife. Kamal and Hassan lived there for a while. Eventually, Hassan brought his family to America and bought a house in a Dallas suburb.

Kamal Ismail, a few years later, married Fatima Hamideh, the daughter of Yusef Hamideh. Yusef Hamideh was the youngest son of Othman Ali Hamideh and his wife, Habiba. Yusef had lived and worked in Fort Worth and Dallas, and eventually he and his entire family moved to Dallas.

As you see, the families are so connected that their story is about each and every one of them.

Some years later, Kamal's brother Ahmed and his wife, Samira, came to America and resided in Dallas. Samira's mother, Iasha, was the daughter of Othman Ali Hamideh. Ahmed also was a skilled tailor and quite successful in his vocation.

After some time, the two youngest Ismail brothers moved to America and were successful entrepreneurs as well. Their names were Mohammed and Awni Ismail. Mohammed married Sawsan Abusaad. The Abusaad family was also from the Lifta village in Palestine. Mohammed Shehadeh Abusaad, Sawson's father, was also from Lifta. He shared the same plight as the other Lifta residents, having to flee to safety for himself and his family. He was also very eager to provide safety for his family.

Like the other Lifta fathers, he wanted a secure life for his family, and education was important in that equation. He became highly successful after having to flee to Jordan. He was initially in the British Jordanian Army. Then, because of his intelligence and acumen, attended a British college in London. He continued on a successful career path and, ultimately, became a consultant to the Secretary of Health in Jordan. His wife was Khadeeja Ahmed Ismail.

All three of these families were very focused not only providing for their families but preparing them with education and/or entrepreneurship.

In totality, each and every single one of these families had to persist through many challenges to achieve success in vocations. If it was becoming educated, becoming entrepreneurs, they were dedicated to whatever hard work it took to provide for their families and create businesses and career paths for all of their progeny.

All three of the families—Hamideh, Ismail, and Abusaad—showed so much persistence to achieve success. And they did.

All of these three Lifta refugee families have gained remarkable achievements in education, entrepreneurship, and community service wherever their paths have taken them.

And the character and examples led by the grandfathers, great grandfathers, and mothers has been nothing short of remarkable. The courage and positive force that they showed after having to flee their homes in Lifta was nothing short of remarkable. They set the bar so high for endurance, faith, and perseverance, and that is why it is so significant for the younger generations and future generations to know the amazing strength of their heritage.

The Lifta Hamideh, Ismail, and AbuSaad legacy is of paramount significance for their descendants and future descendants. The amazing resilience and faith of their forefathers teaches them that steadfast perseverance can and does reward with positive benefits.

Each of these families overcame the highest obstacles and were successful. Each of them reached their entrepreneurship and/or higher educational goals. From becoming small business owners, becoming educators, attorneys, and several other vocations, each of the families leave a legacy. The legacy is that with faith, resilience, hard work, and dedication, you can achieve your goals.

Wherever they live in the world, they continue to leave a mark of distinction. We all can learn from these lessons and strive for the excellence of character that they have shown. That is the Lifta Hamideh, Ismail, and AbuSaad legacy.

The first generations had to reinvent their entire lives more than once, twice, and sometimes even three times. Each of these families were able to accomplish that in a steadfast way.

The legacy from that lives on and is a standard of which each of these families should be proud and keep as a guiding light for generations to come. It is a remarkable legacy for each of these families and for all persons. Faith, perseverance, and resilience are all remarkable qualities that we can see and learn from these generations. The Lifta Hamideh, Ismail, and Abusaad legacy lives on...

"Shaping my Personality and Coming to America"

An Essay by Naji Hamideh

Othman, my father, returned to Palestine from America in 1926. He married Habibah, my mother, in the same year. He started his career by opening a small place to sell produce in Jerusalem. He worked hard, and always had, allowing him to save some money and open a larger place for himself. His business started to progress day by day until it was one of the best. But in 1948, the Palestinian War took place and everything went with the wind. The house that he had established, costing 200,000 dinar, was destroyed, the land was confiscated, and the place was ruined.

This disaster began in 1948, when the war between the Arabs and the Jews broke out. Mind you, 1.5 million refugees, scattering here and there, lived in miserable situations as a result of this war.

* * *

I was born on June 24, 1938, in Lifta, Jerusalem. When I was eight years old, I started to go to an elementary school. When I was in the third grade, we left our home and went to the city where Christ, peace be on his soul, was born in Bethlehem. My father was in a bad condition and my mother was very sick.

In 1950, the second disaster took place: my mother died. I was twelve years old, and my youngest brother was six years old. Her death was a shock to all of us, but nothing can stop God's will.

During the second half of 1950, we moved to Amman, Jordan, searching for a way to make a living. I will never forget the house that we used to live in. It was very small with no kitchen. Six of us lived there.

I spent two years doing nothing but bringing groceries home from the market. Later, I attended an institute that taught mathematics. I spent a year there, then attended one of the best schools in Jordan, Eslamiya Educational College. I liked my school very much because there you could find very religious scholars.

The main purpose of this school was to teach the Islam religion. Being a Muslim, I found complete satisfaction in it. I still remember when we used to go to the mosque and the teacher was our Imam (the person who prays in front of the Muslims). My father used to wake us up at 4 a.m. and say, "It is time to pray, wake up, it is time to pray."

Naji Hamideh and classmates at Islamic Educational College,
a private school in Amman

I graduated from this school in 1958. My favorite subjects during my time studying at this college were religion, Arabic, and English literature. I wasn't good in science because I didn't care about NHy0H or H2S04.

When I graduated, I had an urgent desire to finish college and study economics. I chose the

United States to achieve my goal. I wrote to my oldest brother, who was living in Fort Worth. He sent me an application from TCU. After three weeks, I received my acceptance letter. I started working on attaining my visa, which I got after one month.

Naji Hamideh's brothers Mohammed and Omar in 1952, when Omar took Mohammed to the ship sailing to the United States (he was the first one to come to the United States after his father in 1913 and later returned to Palestine).

It was time to depart from Jordan to America. On January 24, 1958, I was in New York. Twenty-four hours and I was in the second part of the world. I didn't believe it at first, but there was no doubt. I left New York after one day on my way to Fort Worth, which I knew nothing about except that most of the people were cowboys. On the contrary, when I reached Fort Worth on January 26, I found it to be a large, nice, and beautiful city—and I haven't seen a cow for the last six months.

I attended TCU in the spring of 1958. I found myself in a different country but among well-educated citizens. I was classified as a sophomore. I liked America and the American people, and God bless America from sea to shining sea.

"Achievement"

A Poem by Naji Hamideh

Ooh, How sweet is this hour. This hour
when I received the diploma that is the
result of the effort of two years full of
happiness and ease one day and
retractions another day. But hitting the
target (aim) and getting to it takes lots
of effort and staying up late and patience.

As the poet had said: Do not assume that
Glory is Dates you're going to eat, you
will not reach Glory until you taste
bitter cactus (Patience).

About the Author

Sue Nodler Hamideh has lived in Texas for fifty-five years. She was born in Urbana, Illinois and was the first child of Charles Edward Nodler and Beatrice June Beals.

She attended elementary, junior high, and the tenth grade of high school in Champaign, Illinois. Then, her father's job moved the family to southwest Missouri. The resided in Neosho, Missouri and she graduated from Neosho High School. She then attended the University of Arkansas and graduated with a Bachelor of Arts in economics and sociology in 1967.

She had a job offer in Washington DC with the Department of Commerce, Census Bureau, in the Industry Division. She stayed one year and then went home to Missouri. After ten days or so, she drove to Texas to visit her sister and brother-in-law. After a short time, she and her sister decided to take temporary jobs in retail. That changed for Sue, as the company offered her a management training position.

This became a life-changing event, as she met her future husband a few days later. He was already working in management there. His name was Naji Othman Ali Hamideh. They married and have three children and five grandchildren, of which they are most proud.